W9-BBI-167

ANN MORRIS

◆◆◆

ON THE GO

PHOTOGRAPHS BY KEN HEYMAN

LOTHROP, LEE & SHEPARD BOOKS
NEW YORK

Photograph at bottom of page 16 courtesy of Jayce Fox.
Photographs pages 27-29 courtesy of NASA.

Text copyright © 1990 by Ann Morris
Photographs copyright © 1990 by Ken Heyman

4   5   6   7   8   9   10

Library of Congress Cataloging in Publication Data was not available in time for publication of this book, but
can now be obtained from either the Publisher or the Library of Congress.
ISBN 0-688-06336-5   ISBN 0-688-06337-3 (lib. bdg.)
LC Number: 90-33842

All over the world
people move from place to place
carrying babies on their backs,

6   baskets over their shoulders,

and almost anything on their heads. 7

They travel on foot.
They ride on horses and donkeys

and camels.   9

Wheels make things go easier and faster.

They can be pedaled
or pushed…

12   or pulled by ponies

or oxen...

14   or people.

Some wheels are powered by motors. 15

A fire engine hurries
to put out the fire.

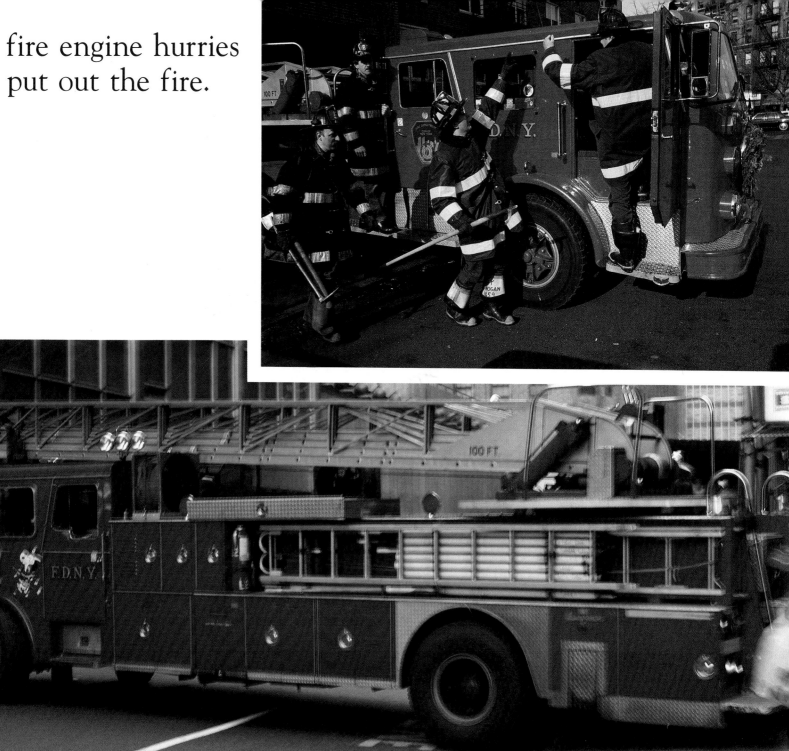

Buses carry people all over town.

18   All aboard! Trains switch from track to track.

A trolley moves
on rails along
the city street.

Zoom!
You can go
150 miles an hour
on a monorail.

People travel on water, too.
Some row their boats.

Others push them along with poles.

Some people sell refreshments from their boats.   21

22   Sailors hope for a good wind.

Tugboats guide ships
from all over
the world
into the harbor.

23

Jet planes carry people and cargo across continents.

26   You can go straight up in a helicopter

or a rocket....Liftoff!

Maybe one day
you will travel to the moon.

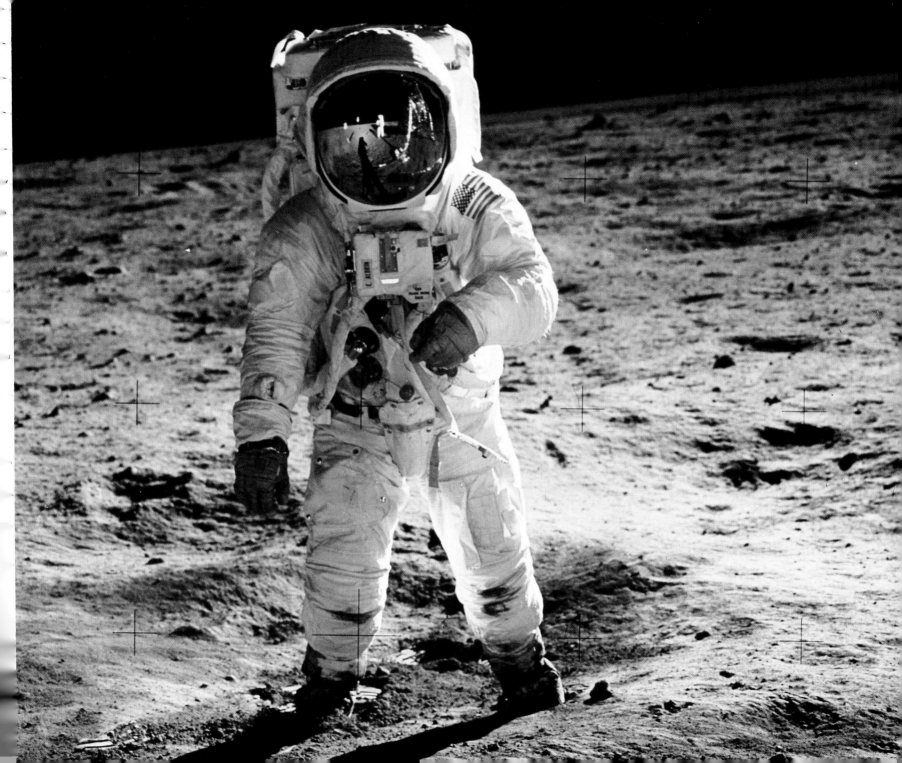

INDEX

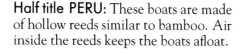

15 GERMANY: You can get a good view of Berlin from the top deck of this double-decker bus.

16 UNITED STATES: Most fire engines in North America are painted red so that people will notice them and get out of their way.

17 EGYPT: A bus station in Cairo. All the city buses start from here.

18 DENMARK: Trains are switched from one track to another, depending on where they are bound. A person inside the little house controls the switches.

19 GERMANY: The poles on top of trolleys are connected to cables, which supply the electricity to power the trolleys.

19 UNITED STATES: This monorail at Disneyland gives visitors a bird's-eye view of the park.

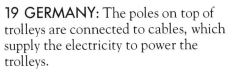

20 SOMALIA: This bargelike boat ferries people across the shallow water. The boatman pushes the craft with his long pole.

21 HONG KONG: In this port where many people live in houseboats, a "restaurant boat" comes to their doors to sell refreshments.

22 AUSTRALIA: This sailing vessel is used for deep-sea clamming.

23 UNITED STATES (both photos): Barges and ocean liners are difficult to maneuver in a city harbor, so tugboats are used to tow or guide them into port.

24 GERMANY: A jet is loaded with cargo before takeoff.

26 UNITED STATES: Helicopters can be used for police work, news reporting, traffic control, or simply for a good view of the city.

27 UNITED STATES: *Apollo 11* lifts off, carrying crew and scientific instruments beyond the earth.

28–29 THE MOON: An astronaut walks near his lunar module.

Where in the world were these photographs taken?

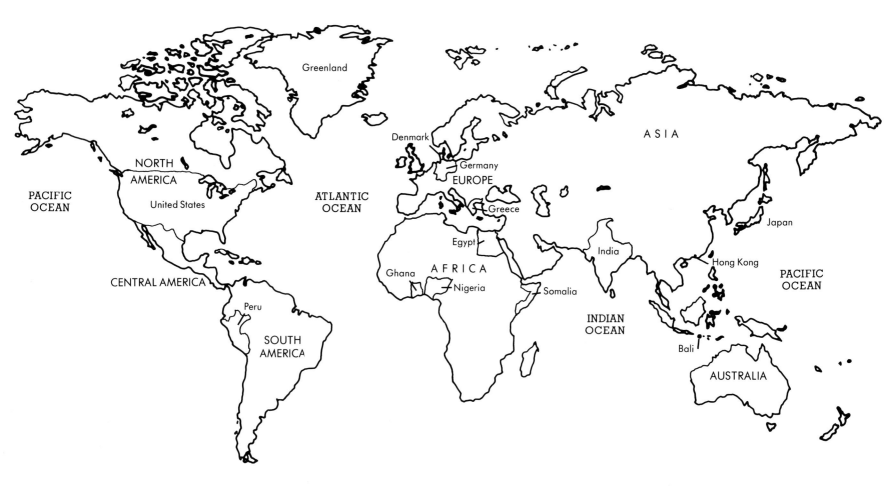

Greenland

Denmark

Germany

EUROPE

Greece

ASIA

Japan

PACIFIC
OCEAN

NORTH
AMERICA

United States

ATLANTIC
OCEAN

Egypt

Ghana

AFRICA

Nigeria

Somalia

India

Hong Kong

PACIFIC
OCEAN

CENTRAL AMERICA

Peru

SOUTH
AMERICA

INDIAN
OCEAN

Bali

AUSTRALIA